CLEMENTI

SIX SONATAS OPUS 4 FOR THE PIANO

Erroneously known as SIX SONATINAS, Op. 37 & Op. 38

PRACTICAL PERFORMING EDITION
EDITED FROM THE ORIGINAL SOURCES BY WILLARD A. PALMER

For over one hundred years Muzio Clementi's *SIX SONATAS, Opus 4,* have been published under the erroneous title *SONATINAS, Opus 37* and *38.* Three of the six "sonatinas" were assigned to each incorrect opus, and in addition to this the order of the first two were reversed. It is difficult to imagine how such errors could be the result of any sort of honest mistake. These works were published during Clementi's lifetime by four different firms including Clementi's own publishing house, each time with the title *SIX SONATAS FOR PIANOFORTE OR HARPSICHORD, OPUS IV.* The date of the first publication was 1780, and the first edition also included an optional part for violin or flute.

One is tempted to suspect that some enterprising individual, noting the unprecedented success of Clementi's *SIX SONATINAS, Opus 36,* decided that a similar title with consecutive opus numbers might be conducive to similar success. The sonatas of Opus 4 were undoubtedly chosen because they are excellent follow-up material for any student who has mastered Opus 36. Because this is true, these sonatas have survived in the teaching repertoire, and still enjoy success that is second only to the famous Sonatinas.

Clementi did actually compose and publish an Opus 37 and an Opus 38. The real Opus 37 consists of three rather difficult sonatas, each with three movements: No. 1 in C Major, No. 2 in G Major and No. 3 in D Major. The real Opus 38 is a collection of twelve original waltzes for pianoforte, tambourine and triangle.

In the present edition, the place of Opus 4 in the original order of the sonatas has been restored. Each sonata consists of two contrasting movements, rather than the three usually found in sonatas cast in classical forms. These works actually fall into the classification of "pre-classical," and the baroque influence, as far as form is concerned, is much in evidence.

(continued on p. 64)

Cover art: Westminster Bridge, London,
    with the Lord Mayor's Procession on the Thames
    by Antonio Canal, called Canaletto (Italian, 1697–1768)
    Oil on canvas, 1747 (95.75 x 127.5 cm)
    Yale Center for British Art
    Paul Mellon Collection, New Haven

Sonata No. 1
in D Major

Opus 4
Muzio Clementi

(a) Played: Similarly in measures 3, 5, 9, 11, etc.

(b) This and similar trills in this movement begin on the upper note.

(c) The wedge-shaped staccato mark, according to Clementi's *Introduction to the Art of Playing on the Pianoforte,* simply indicates a very short staccato, a bit shorter than that indicated by the dot. It does not imply any special stress or emphasis.

(d) This trill begins on the upper note.

4

(e) The *short appoggiaturas* are played very quickly, on the beat.

(f) These trills (here and in measures 61 and 64) begin on the upper note.

ⓖ This trill begins on the upper note.

Menuetto

ⓐ This is a long appoggiatura, played:

ⓑ The trills, here and in measure 19, begin on the upper note.

Menuetto da capo, senza replica

Sonata No. 2
In E♭ Major

ⓐ Played: ⓑ Played: ⓒ Played:

ⓓ The wedge, according to Clementi's *Introduction to the Art of Playing on the Pianoforte,*
simply indicates a short staccato. It does not imply any special stress or emphasis.

ⓔ The trill begins on the upper note.

(f) The short appoggiaturas are played very quickly, on the beat of the following note.

(g) This trill may begin on the principal note.

10

ⓗ This and similar trills in this movement begin on the upper note.

(i) This symbol ⌇, as used here, represents a three-note *transient trill*:

(a) This trill may be played as a *transient trill*, beginning on the principal note.

18

ⓑ This trill may be played as a *transient trill*, beginning on the principal note.

Sonata No. 3
In C Major

(b) Here the symbol ᴧᴧ indicates a three note *transient trill:* ♪♪♪ or ♪♪♪. Measure 89 is similarly played.

ⓒ The short appoggiaturas are played very quickly, on the beat.
ⓓ This trill begins on the upper note. A turn may be substituted for simplification, if desired.
ⓔ This trill begins on the upper note.
ⓕ This trill begins on the upper note. A turn may be substitued for simplification, if desired.

(g) This trill begins on the upper note.

(h) This trill begins on the upper note. For simplification, a turn may be substituted.

(i) This trill begins on the upper note.

(j) This trill begins on the upper note. For simplification, a turn may be substituted.

ⓐ The short appoggiaturas are played very quickly, on the beat.

ⓑ In this and similar measures, the symbol ᴧᴧ may be interpreted as the three-note transient trill, beginning on the main note, played ⟨figure⟩ or ⟨figure⟩

Ⓒ This trill begins on the upper note.

ⓓ This trill begins on the upper note.

(e) This trill begins on the upper note.

(g) Each of these trills begins on the upper note.

Sonata No. 4
In G Major

(a) The wedge, according to Clementi's *Introduction to the Art of Playing on the Pianoforte*, simply indicates a short staccato. It does not imply any special stress or emphasis.

(b) This trill and the one in the following measure should begin on the upper note.

Ⓒ This trill and the following one (measure 40) should begin on the upper note.
The trills in measures 85 and 87 are similar.

ⓓ Played:

Tempo di Menuetto
Andantino

ⓐ These are short appoggiaturas, and should be played very quickly, on the beat.

ⓑ This trill, because it is played legato with the preceding upper second, may begin on the principal note.

ⓒ This trill should begin on the upper note.

(d) This trill may begin on the principal note.

(e) These trills should begin on the upper note.

(f) This trill may begin on the principal note.

Sonata No. 5
In B♭ Major

ⓐ   This trill should begin on the upper note:

(b) The wedge indicates a short staccato, and implies no special stress or emphasis. The dot over the first note of the measure indicates that the note is less staccato than those with wedges. These are rules from Clementi's *Art of Playing on the Pianoforte*.

(c) This trill begins on the upper note. Measure 98 is similar.

(d) Played:: [musical notation] or [musical notation] Measures 42, 100, 102, 108 and 110 have trills that are similarly played.

(e) Played: [musical notation]

(f) This trill begins on the upper note. The trill in measure 122 is similarly played.

(g) Played: [musical notation] The short appoggiaturas in measures 60, 124 and 126 are similarly played.

(h) This trill begins on the upper note. The trill in measure 82 is similar.

① This trill begins on the upper note.

Rondo
Allegretto

ⓐ This trill begins on the upper note.

ⓑ This trill begins on the upper note.

© This is a trill with a prefix and suffix, commonly played on such fermatas as this one.

It is played approximately:  The number of

(a piacere)

repercussions depends entirely on the whim of the performer, since the trill may be sustained for any reasonable length of time, as the fermata indicates.

Sonata No. 6
In F Major

(a) The trills, here and in measure 31, should begin on the upper note.

(b) Played:

(d)   The first of the three small notes should be played on the beat.

(e)   This may be regarded as a three-note transient trill, beginning on the principal note,

played:

(f)   The small notes should be played as 16th notes, on the beat of the following note.

(g)   This trill begins on the upper note.

ⓐ The short appoggiaturas are played very quickly, on the beat.

ⓑ This trill begins on the upper note.

© This trill begins on the upper note.

(d) This trill begins on the upper note.

Suggestions for the performance of all the ornaments is provided in footnotes by the present editor. These recommendations are based on a careful study of Clementi's *INTRODUCTION TO THE ART OF PLAYING ON THE PIANOFORTE,* the most widely used method book of its time, first published in 1801. This method was recommended by Beethoven, even as late as 1826, and was possibly used by Chopin. It saw at least 11 editions, some "with great improvements by the author," and its influence on style and performance surpassed any other instruction book of its day.

The following observations, derived from Clementi's method, should be particularly noted:

TRILLS

Clementi preferred the upper note start for most trills. When the trilled note was immediately preceded by the upper 2nd, and legato was indicated, he allowed a principal note start, but even in such cases his own indicated fingering shows that he frequently began such trills on the upper note. The short trill indicated by the sign ∿ was, particularly in rapid descending passages played as a three-note transient trill, beginning on the main note. But even this sign was often used to indicate the short trill beginning on the upper note.

APPOGGIATURAS

Small notes indicating long and short appoggiaturas were played on the beat of the following large note. The only exceptions here are those small notes which serve as terminations for trills.

STACCATO

Clementi used three different kinds of staccato indications

1. The wedge ♪ ♪ ♪

   indicates that the note should be instantly released

2. The dot ♪ ♪ ♪

   indicates less staccato than the preceding sign.

3. The slur and dot ♪ ♪ ♪

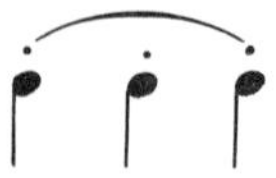

   indicates still less staccato.

It is important to note that the wedge did not imply any special stress or accent, as it sometimes does in later music and it is often used on notes that are played very softly.

LEGATO

Clementi was one of the first of the school of "legato pianists," and is regarded as one of the founders of the style of playing that stressed the importance of the long legato line.

This tradition of playing was carried on by Beethoven, who had the highest regard for Clementi's abilities, both as a performer and as a composer.

PEDALING

The original edition of these sonatas contains no pedal indications. There is no doubt that judicious use of the damper pedal would add to the effectiveness of many measures. Care should be taken that no pedaling interferes with the phrasing and staccato indications provided by the composer.